PRAISE FOR *LUNG HOURS*

In Jessica Purdy's *Lung Hours*, the dialectic and the lyric are wound around each as if copper wire were laced through the body's vascular system, where the hard lived wisdom and bodily betrayal of middle age are struck through by the lightning strike of language and image. Here is a study of the fragile skein of family and womanhood as well a deep meditation on the nature of being as Purdy moves through and gets stuck inside of time: "Say you're skipping now/ the way you used to as a child. /Who are you exactly anymore?" And ever hanging over the poems are the questions of how our selves change over a life and how do we reconcile with the selves we were, and the selves we yet hope to be: "When/ I thought I knew myself I was a period at the end of a/ sentence. I was never a question. Until I was." Collected here are poems that at once delight us with surprises of language, of line, of sentence, of syntax and then suddenly stop us with the cold breath of haunted spaces and the poltergeist of memory. And yet there is, as the title suggests, ever a space to dream, to breathe, to love, and to repair the reaving of each day. I've long been a fan of Purdy's work and *Lung Hours* may be my favorite book of hers so far.

—Matt Miller
Author of *Tender the River* (Texas A&M University Press)

Lung Hours

Published by Gunpowder Press
Edited by David Starkey and Chryss Yost
PO Box 60035
Santa Barbara, CA 93160-0035

Front cover image: "Woman in Profile with Flowers"
by Odilon Redon (1840-1916)

Author photo: Mae Schneider

ISBN-13: 978-1-957062-29-7
Library of Congress Control Number: 2026903749

www.gunpowderpress.com

Gunpowder Press is part of Gunpowder Poetry, a 501(c)(3) nonprofit literary organization. The Dryden-Vreeland Book Prize honors two high school teachers, Michael Dryden and Susan Vreeland, who were influential in lives of Gunpowder's editors. The prize is awarded for an exceptional manuscript of poems by a poet working in K-12 education.

Lung Hours

Poems

Jessica Purdy

Gunpowder Press • Santa Barbara
2026

*This book is for
my children Jack and Mae,
and my husband Paul*

CONTENTS

I.

II.

III.

IV.

V.

This is the lung-tree.
These orchids are splendid. They spot and coil like snakes.
The heart is a red-bell-bloom, in distress.
I am so small
In comparison to these organs!
I worm and hack in a purple wilderness.

—Sylvia Plath
excerpt from "The Surgeon at 2 A.M."

I.

I like to ride on things that shouldn't be ridden

At the rodeo I volunteered to be thrown off the donkey. The clown led
the audience in mocking my fall. How could I blame him? I hid inside the
mouth of the big yellow demolition machine and rode it down into the
abandoned house. Together we bit into the neon green *Fuck Bitches* graffiti
on the old living room's sheetrock. It's okay because my hands are too soft to
crush anything alive or dead. We tore its bones out and the insulation came
up pink and frothing like lungs. The sun was hot on the top of my head,
and the birds didn't know what to do with this new information. They were
flying so small and panicked. Dozens of trees lay hacked to death. Vines
had tried a kind of embrace. I've ridden the Ferris Wheel hanging by my
sweaty knees. I had to rely on my body to hold me. My hair hung down and
tangled in the wind and the lights of this town. The muddy ground was
littered with wrappers and cups. I'm always trying to ride a bicycle at night.
I've figured out how to lie down and look at the stars while pedaling. The
path so familiar, I navigate by sound and sky. It's the old neighborhood and
nothing can harm me.

Sometimes You Wake from Unnerving Dreams

Ones where you've taken out your own eyeballs and teeth,
mixed them up in a bowl as if they're soup.

The blue irises like shriveled birthday balloons.
They are detached from you.

No longer set in your face. The face you've seen in mirrors your whole life.
Miraculous. You can still see without them. Still chew food.

Sometimes you wake and the face of the land has changed.
Snow fell in the night.

A forest that was brown and green just yesterday is now gray and white.
Flakes melt into the soup of the river that runs to your own house.

Sometimes you wake and it's still night. You can't see anything but your thoughts,
the rectangle of light near the ceiling.

Sleep is where you belong. Sleep is where you just were,
but something woke you. You wonder what woke you.

Just yesterday you were thudding over pine-needled ground,
over hemlock roots and dropped cones. The hollow sound of underground space.

You might trip looking up. Asking questions:
What kind of bird builds such a big nest?

Will this really be the year you can stop worry? Did you take a wrong turn
or is this way home equally good?

You need to discern whether you've seen that fern before,
that mossy rock with miniature worlds.

Sometimes you wake and the face of the land has changed.
Snow fell in the night.

You need to eat a meal that sustains you, teeth firmly rooted in your jaw.

Ouroboros

Beginnings are snowscapes. Or skin
never touched by the sun until birth.

The end of a year is just as cheek-slapped
as its opposite. In spring we wait.

Like ice grits its teeth and succumbs
to melting. New England summers

that used to feel yearslong only relax
the shoulders. Fleeting as foxes.

Summer runs through the yard. Robins
fight circles in the hedges. Black-striped

eyes and black coats with red epaulets
cling to the cattails. Songs never heard

before emerge. Yelling with the whole
body. Sense the warnings. You are not

welcome in their world. Three sparrows
hold the iron patio furniture as if

they might lift off and take the chairs
in their claws. Dandelions bloom yellow

forever until they turn white from sorrow
overnight. Why aren't there fish visiting

the forests? Dirigibles navigating the air
as if they could breathe there? Why was

childhood an eternity? Yes, there were
fireflies and kerosene lamps. On the round

kitchen table, oilcloth spread. Bare feet
grasping the wooden rungs of mismatched

chairs. Our bodies so flexible we'd compare
who could bend to bite their own toenails.

Why was childhood an eternity? That salty,
dirty, sweat-on-the-tongue ending.

Worm Moon

She sees the moon as her own retina. Galaxies
are her eyes. She wakes with a coyote
claw whipping into her mouth.

Wind cannot move the moon
that hooks the edge of her blind.
She tastes the dirt inside

the ridged keratin, the bone
of bleached knuckle. Sucks her lip—
a worm between her teeth. Spits.

Things sing in the stubborn trees.
Vernal pools spawn hysterical quacks.
Ducks or frogs? Their rituals

urge her through mud season, fog sizzling
in the pan at dawn. Nothing that hides
can be frazzled, her own body fuzzy

as it thaws. Mist clings in her branches.
She's dripping. Leaves tracks she doesn't recognize.
She's got her own claws. Who'll hear

her howl tonight and wonder
where the woman went? Anyone
studying the moon could find her.

Daybreak

I'm walking to the beach, getting blood
to pump through my legs, the veins

and capillaries sing with plasma; autonomic
clock of heart, drop of foot.

My concerns drift as if they can be suspended
before day shifts. Arrival light until—

I want to pause before the sun blasts
the sky into a squint, feel

dawn hold me in its container,
an open bowl. I could watch

forever—ivy, berries, birds.
A sudden coyote on the yellow lines.

My fear is holding me.
I can wait, imagine where that beast goes

after scaling the sand dune
and vanishing. Murky and gray, heathered,

grainy as old silent films. Now
the clouds seep with raspberry juice;

now I'm running to water; the layered east
coloring the vapor so sweet

I slip into the dyed red waves.
My body blushes

coral. My heart's a slapping fish, legs
a flipping tail, feet, coyote feet.

Chimera, I flash
in that pink second before earth turns,

pulling the ocean back blue to its chest,
quotidian as a workshirt, or fur, or scales.

I'd Rather Be a Non-Human Animal

Would there always be war? The way the movie plots went
        humans would never decide to live in harmony.
Our suitcases would always be packed for evacuation.

Would there ever be a moving sidewalk,
        a weather control machine
roads that melted snow on impact?

Would children always have to go to school? (watch their mothers bleed)
        Women are better than men at ultramarathons.
As I sleep a headache raps on my skull with its bloody wrench.

The moon casts someone else's daylight and I'm without glasses
        except for the slider door whose glass presents me with an option:
look outside. It should be dark but the moon finds me

bending my neck like a flower to the sun
        so bright I squint
against the urgent yard flooded with blue shadows.

My vestigial tail curled and primed I climb
        the stairs and consider the learning curve it will take
to transition my coccyx to walking on all fours.

I am patient. I have the endurance of starlight.
        My sleep the texture of a fossilized nautilus.
My body has done what it wants.

It even folded its dirty feathers against the mountain ridge of my spine.
        Why not? Considering what humanity is capable of
I take the shape of water and seep through the cracks.

Sleeping Over for the First Time

At Darcy's after watching *King Kong*
he came to the window. My mind
so worked up I couldn't stay.
I knew my own bed was just across
the dirt road where we played Skip-it
and climbed crabapple trees all day.
Like Peter Rabbit we pushed the boundaries
of adult properties. I would've sat
munching thistle all day in that garden.
McGregor had long arms and an old boat
for a planter that spilled out zinnias.
We must've watched the black and white movie
after dinner where I told Darcy's parents
I loved broccoli and made them believe
me by eating it all up. I don't remember
watching it, but I remember his eyes
in the window after. He could reach right
in and pluck me. Something so big
could cover a lot of ground in a few
short steps. Climb the side of a house
to the window to look in on my nightdress,
seafoam green with a ruffled
edge I loved to spin and watch flare.
The neighbor boys would burn ants
with the lasered sun through a magnifying glass.
My mother told me: Stay away from him
he's fresh. Gypsy moth caterpillars
shimmied up the trees and tented them.
The sting of a sunburn would slowly build
after the longest beach day. Burns that heated

the coolest sheets as I tried to sleep.
Tomatoes from the patio planters picked
like little suns still warm, warmed
even my hot hands. Darcy's dad was nice.
Didn't deserve to be stung on the tongue by a bee
he didn't see sitting on the Oreo
he'd popped in his mouth. Her mom
called my mom and I felt so ashamed
I'd failed at the slumber party. Went
home in the dark. It rained and
rain just made the giant's fur glitter.

As Ann Darrow

Too many hanging grapes
and gauzy dresses kept me
admiring my own face
in the mirror. I was so small
I could be pocketed. Palmed.
Belly poked. Pout and smile

paint and highlight. What did
men want from me? I gave
and gave. Never knowing
the pedestal's chains held
my wrists so tightly
I wanted more. What animals

men are. Sniffing around my neck
inside my eardrums.
I'd withstand drips of saliva
to have them worship me.
Nevermind their faces were giant
and pockmarked. Fingertips

as big as my abdomen. Reeking
of whatever they were drinking
I'd lay my ear against their chests
to hear the speed of their blood.
As if maybe I'd hear the monster in them dying.
As if maybe that would show I'd cared.

The Elephant's Child

"Go to the banks of the great grey-green, greasy Limpopo River, all set about with fever-trees, and find out."
                                          —Rudyard Kipling

On Cape Cod even rocks have a scent. Resonant as if the sun is distilled within them. I'm here now. There's this wooden ladder become part of the earth on its side at the top of a hill near hydrangeas. The sandy, random way things fall. The scrub pines' fragrant too, and spongy deadfall. Ferns curled and browning. Something scuttles in the underbrush. Sunned skin and moss. Each turn a new vibration. Each flutter. I smell the wood of childhood, the scent of damp lichen breathing its lacy life. When I was a girl I kept my perfect fingernails in a box in my vanity. My red bathing suit felt like my idea of a woman. I could see my chest emerging from its flat landscape. Things I could not name, telltale flicker of bird. My feet bare. It was summer. Some days we didn't go to the beach, we were bored enough to count cars as they went by, drink from the garden hose's metallic cold through the hot afternoon. In the bathroom, Jergens stung. My nightgown was a filmy pale ghost that twirled as I spun. I'd read Just So Stories and feel strange moral feelings in my body. I reached for understanding, the words seemed old-fashioned and instructive. Was I the right audience? The book stayed in the summer house and each year I'd read musty pages, damp and warped. The rocker held me fast until I rocked too hard and fell backward. I crashed, hitting my head. The blood that came contained mythology— blue until the air turned it red. I dreamed someday I would buy my own red bathing suit and the chest would rise as high as Farrah Fawcett's, but in the meantime I'd tuck my knees up under my shirt from my perch on the stairs imagining what I'd like to become—Kipling's great grey-green greasy Limpopo River rolling through my mind like music. Like a bird I still can't name, its yellow wings whistling through branches that wind has left to rest where they fell.

When You Start Running at 51

In the year I start running the killdeer raise their young
blocking the track and screaming at me. My legs separate
from my eyes which are drawn to their black neck rings.
Sometimes I run as fast as I can and feel like I might lift
off, explode like a failed rocket and fall down. My shirt
would streak with red rubber. They'd peel the lane numbers
off me at the coroner's. Because honestly how many more
years will my joints keep pistoning me forward? When
I thought I knew myself I was a period at the end of a
sentence. I was never a question. Until I was. The mark
stamped on my skull like a missed lesson. A schoolbook
weighs me down in my backpack I sling over one shoulder
some days and I just want to examine the cones
of the echinacea plants. Their shimmer nears me to bee-
status: all hum and business. This week in the year
I started running the chicken thighs went rancid
and the bread sprung up white spots two days after
I brought it home. I've been thinking at bedtime
about how easy it would be to succumb to poppy
sleep. How much I want that letting go of the dust
on my nightstand, the toenail clippings someone left
in the carpet. I'd be a junky and fall in love
with my bed. I've still so much left to read. Why can't
I remember any of the words? When I walk the track
with my husband he talks about living somewhere
that doesn't get so cold in the winter. It's then that
the floor falls away inside the house of my insides.
Though I know what he means, how the broken asphalt
in our driveway can lead to this dawning. Our lives of cracking
foundations and flooded basements. I'm moving further

toward lunatic. The one the town kids know as the crazy lady.
Don't look her in the eye, she's looking for attention.
I'm running across the green fields and screaming
at threats to my children even though they're as grown
as me. Funny little legs and feet that touch the ground.
My arms pinioned. My throat ringed as double-dark
as an obsidian choker that tightens. That old sensation
just before the sharp spring of tears comes to the eye.

There is Nothing Not with Me Anymore

Memory flicks its tail. Disappears behind rocks. Memory has this brown fur. *What was that?* Someone asks. The answer is one of three things, though I'll never be sure which one it is

definitively. At my kitchen window where I've stood every day I see the pussy willows are beginning to burst open into leaves. As they did last year. The dusty screen in the window is like

time. This build up of dust makes it hard to see out. What use is all this time anyway? The seeds sprouted while I wasn't looking. Now it's spent wondering when to transplant. I'm no gardener

but I can push a seed into dirt. Make it disappear. The seeds were dry, white, hard. The soil is dark and stinks of the earth's breath. What wonder appears on the seventh day. Memory

entrusted to time rises, unfurling, pushing its tender arms toward the sun. Some don't ever come back up, they're like stones thrown deep into a summer lake. Submerged like this, the

stones become slippery, furred with algae. The water's displacement is barely discerned, but can be measured over time—retreating marks of detritus where it once touched the shore.

Say Memories are Current Events

Say you're nearing the woods
and a fly begins to bother you.
Returning again and again
despite your waving it away
and you are walking alone
on the dirt road
no one around to see you dance
to the music in your ears. Say
you're skipping now
the way you used to as a child.
Who are you exactly anymore?
Say you're traveling further
and further away from
the delinquent water bill.
The windows that need replacing.
Your children and their serious
troubles. Say you forgot to wear
bug spray. Say you can't see
in the woods once you reach them
because you're wearing sunglasses.
Say you feel joy despite all the aches.
The people you miss. Who do you miss?
Who are you yearning for?
Say you learned a childhood friend
has died unexpectedly.
Does that make you wonder
how despair might have been filling
him? His sad eyes look out
from his obituary and you can't
remember what he looked like

in high school. Only that he was kind
to you then. Say you're now hearing
a melody that makes your feet stomp
the muddy path like you're
in Flashdance. The 80s far
in the rearview but so close you can
touch the air between you
and your classmates. The desks
and melamine chairs. The chalkboard
dust and summer air coming
through the tilt-out windows
just before school lets out on the last day.
Say you didn't know then
that you would ever dream
that you couldn't find your classroom.
Never attend the class at all and yet
you have to take the test
without knowing a damn thing.
All the hallways are long and lockered
and then you're outside on the other end
of a campus you don't have a map for
and the stairs back are in some hidden
part of the school getting smaller
and smaller as you try to find your way.
Say you wake up relieved that this
never really happened to you.
The bathtub soap scum is yours.
The windows still open and shut
even if sometimes you can't see
through them. The water still runs
in the sink and you use it to wash
your face, your hands. The same

face you've always had. Your throat
looks saggier now than when
you were young and wore eyeshadow
that matched your nail polish.
Blue mascara. Feathered your hair.
Under the green of trees, say you fear
you won't hear the coyotes
triangulating around you, the rabid
fox who might enter from out of nowhere
but you leave it. Just leave it behind
like the rest of the normal people
who live like they own
everything they touch. Say you can
pretend like that for these few
precious minutes until you're galloping
again, the drumbeat in your ears
lifting your heart so high it is your chest
pulling you along. Say you can feel it
strung like there's a kite attached up there.
Somewhere you can't see,
but in your mind it's old-school:
diamond-shaped, bright yellow,
and neatly tied with a bow.

If I Could I'd See the Northern Lights on a Sunday Night
During Intermission

A piano plays in Iceland. No background noise of football fans
tinny in the evening living room.
Maybe a throat clears and I excuse myself from the theater
escape out the loading zone doors
and place my gloved hands on the steel railing
lift one foot to toe the galvanized nubs.
Green gauze curtains folded over gods and goddesses.
If I could hear the lights' muffled song.
No snap of sun to sear the retinas.
Nor your doldrum of insurance payments.
Galaxies exist, blood vessel tributaries
and spots of nebulas still burning their exits out.
The aurora borealis paints itself
like mountainsides in spring.
A trick of the mind—water flowing purple to red. I'm wandering
wearing yellow-tinted glasses,
framing my Sundays in these keys of velvet black.

Know-It-All

The cat sleeps in the sunspot. The heat wilts
the strawberry plant with its bumper crop
of candy red drops. From here they resemble
hearts. The sunflower wilts. Do know-it-alls
get tired of themselves? There should be a flower
named the Know-It-All, who is secretly
jealous of anything answering "I don't know."
There are people whose take on the world
is to take on the world's problems. I'm asking
for your good news. I wish I was so brave, but I know
what isn't good for me: Whatever boils to the top
and needs skimming. The foul breath
of standing water. The simmering mosquito
larvae I half want to poison, half want to watch
transform into flight. My pretties! I escape
the heat in hemlocks and white pines.
The forest is its own camouflage. In the last
heat of summer every root tries to grab hold.
Each moving thing tries to be birthed. What is at stake
for me when so many are suffering? I can
love the Norway Spruce's weeping branches.
I can place my hands on the wall with
my eyes closed. Try desperately to recall all
the lines in *The Props assist the house*. Here
is where I remember elementary school.
The teacher's lounge plumed
with cigarette smoke. How they allowed
us to smoke in the courtyard of the high
school. How free the teachers seemed.
Gathering in meetings cooled by the only

air conditioner. Their lunches, how lucky!
Their platters of donuts and cupcakes.
How selfish we are, all of us broken.
I don't know why some of us
are destined to be dishes thrown
as if intended for mosaics. I don't know why
some of us live like the hardened floor
the pieces shatter against, scatter over.

You Can Catch More Flies with Honey than with Vinegar

And I'm caught. Lured by the smell of rotting fruit
I creep in smiling. My feet stick. Just a fly.

When I was young how could I know the oak gall
came from a wasp laying her eggs?
Am I even old enough to have learned anything from
my mistakes? I'd pick them up and press my thumbs in
rip them apart expecting sweetness

getting dried chambers instead. A birthplace.
When I last saw my grandfather he called me a different name.
This was how I knew I wouldn't see him again.
Younger I was so wise. Now I can't tell at all if

I'll see the ones I love again. The honeybee on
the dandelion, his pockets full of gold
I worry will seep herbicide into the comb
kill the queen.
Smoke will sleep them into compliance. The keeper

encased in classic white
protection readies the ladder
to retrieve the swarm high up in the oak.
Vision—a bridal veil—blurs, tucked in at the throat.
Heels caught in the branches. Silk rips.
Stung lips and their pout.
I have been ungrateful—
sour and fermented. A goiter. Any growth
a growth borne of assumption.

In spring a spider and her silk egg sac pour
out of the spigot
and into my watering can.
She isn't stupid. Just unwise.

Mystery Speaks

I'm just out of reach, on the periphery,
a shaking branch, a darting shape
like someone touching your right elbow
from behind in a crowd. You turn to see
who it was but I'm gone. On the subway,
I've kept alive a daffodil wrapped
in damp paper towel and tinfoil. Maybe
you've seen my tan suede boots, the way
they make you think of the soft spring
calf and her mother. Could be my yellow
dress that stuns you, makes you lose
your train of thought. The engine of my
heart hidden deep underground.
The tunnel and its track and us
lumbering along sometimes for years,
and you're searching for clues. The veins
in my hands, the fingers that clench
the scrunched foil, the papery skin
of the flower, the green stem. How I
sway with the subway's rumble,
stumble, and clutch the handlebar
to steady myself. You've put out ads
in missed connections to find me, papered
telephone poles and the cork boards
of coffee houses with my last known
whereabouts. Consulted psychics. Kept
notes on every voice message. Hung string
to show the interconnecting points
of knowledge. Your shoes have grown
thin against the pavement. The daffodils
have gone into hiding. After all
this time, you still remember me.
How you loved the way my boots fit my feet
so much that you never saw my face.

She-Hulk

"Anger is a short madness"
—Horace

When She-Hulk says she has already learned how to control her anger
just by being a woman walking down the street
I laugh, make a note in the room. The air between me
and my husband hangs heavy with my silent "see what I mean."

No, he can never see what I mean, though I try to make him
remember all the times I stuck my head into the wind
and yelled back or shrunk to half my size just to make sure
I could stay in the room. Getting bigger and angrier
and greener won't help. *Spandex is your friend*, Hulk advises She-Hulk.

First there was Hulk. Then the female version. Women know
the female's anger came first. She just learned to hide it better.
It snaked into her veins. She slept with one finger on the trigger,
the other stopped the flow of milk to her breast.

I've called attention to my lips. Slept heavily on exhaustion. Even so,
I woke with gratitude in the soles of my feet. You know resentment
can live in your physical body. Is this why it hurts to be human? Sorry,
I meant woman. See any girl and think how her body can be entered.
No matter how locked. She can't get away.

I don't know if anger is green. For me it's the purple of engorgement.
It's the black phone in the hall. The rapist's voice inside it mindless
as a thumb clicking a pen. And the voice coming from you
is only just realizing what he's done to it forever. The voice that wants
to smash the receiver against the wall just to shove your pain into his ear further.

Yes, that's my voice. There's no air behind it. It's his anger that gets to breathe.

II.

One Hundred Percent Effaced

—after Plath's "The Detective"

Are you children with me?
My wheat smell. My eye shape.
I've noticed false teeth in a voice.

Do you know today I said
Sorry babies to the birds. Saw
a hand-sized hyacinth as evidence of a slap.

Vacationed in anger. Lusted after
myself. Hidden my knees. Stalked
the grass for mushrooms and frogs. Fingered

dewy plastic toys in the dirt. Doll parts and mother-
of-pearl grips. Whatever was forgotten from my
childhood. Puckered my lips to fill

my stomach now effaced as an empty thrift store purse.
Crepe paper clutch. Deflated balloon. Rubber skin
a mask I smiled. I tucked my fears

into your cribs and ran fast
up the stairs. Worried my forehead

full of gunshots. Bodies who've called to come identify.
Can you ever know me now I'm gone?

lover lover over and over

this morning of the sixth day of illness there's so much I'm missing and this bird outside singing lover lover over and over and I don't know who is singing it sighing it like we can just repeat ourselves replicate in terms of devotion of nest building of songs that flirt or warn or chide when all night the rain poured onto my floor as I slept and fever sweat poured out of my body into cotton nightclothes and I dreamed of recliners and cars parked just so others could inch by and one driver decided she'd make the others wait and wait and she didn't care and dug in her heels and the recliner was also a vehicle and I decided I didn't want to listen to that woman in the dream anymore and woke up to this bird I can't name by its song all this emerging I'm missing this warmth the kind that's new in April and haven't I seen this green before this winging past my window this daytime moon and nights of rain and still what wouldn't I have had I not been through it the days marked by hyping and dancing and shouting where is that bird I can only hear I look to the trees and the sun glares off the windows clouds cover over this haze in a fevered mind forgetting what it's like to notice the feathers that make me want to be a better person loss of taste and smell but still there's a feeling of smell a sweetness on the part of the tongue that lets you know you're still in a world you can recognize despite the losses

Gizzard Brain

—after "Heaven and Its Orange Flowers" by Mary Biddinger

I pulled from my skull a dead baby head
a broken ornament with mossy eyes.

Are you my ghost, teratoma pulled from the hair
behind my ear, follicle like a hornet hole?

Shrunken as a raisin, the bones beneath wax.
Teeth bared as in one who sleeps unaware

through the burning toaster
the lists of responsibilities.

Love you, Mom, a birthday greeting
and one shelf down it's only women who create people.

It's mothers who are to blame for everything.
Grandma had this same "twin theory" cyst.

In the dusty basement of my ghost
the root of evil humped up out of the concrete.

I asked my ghost if it could lift today's cement
clouds like rusty gym equipment.

Inexplicably then, my old friend's baby drew green circles
on a floor lined as paper notebooks are.

If my ghost was dangled like a bulb from a strand of keratin
sebum squeezed from pores like mini skin cell graves.

I thought my ghost would like me better
than to give me a tumor I regurgitate like a pellet from the

owl I am. All that let me survive has passed through me.
I'm captivated by night's arrangement.

Remembering My Grandmother's Table

Six cotton flowers looking for a way to keep living
behind glass, bob their brainy heads. The black cat

misses his calling as the mouse escapes
under the tablecloth's long skirt. Which way is out?

Says the window: *Why is it night and half of me is dark?*
Disaster curtains won't let me stay transparent.

There are too many vacuums stored under cover.
Oh stems of neglected time, where are your traumas?

Purple

is round in the mouth
like a plum dusky with mist
on the skin tart and crisp thin
as an elderly bruise under an IV
marking fluid injection
into yellow flesh that pulps
in the teeth. A harp plucked
and dragged with spirits says
there's golden light and juice
to miss once you're gone.
The blush-blue crepe
of a grandmother's chest
in your memory. Like film of her
a ghost of her voice returning.
And wasn't it always this way?
Where you think you have a grasp
on where your body resides this time.
Where your blood and flesh
makes other blood that could kill you
without a shot in the buttock.
And you are only a summer visitor
in the life you've been given.

What the Red-Spotted Purple Butterfly Brought

In the window though, it isn't a butterfly wing.
It might be the sun through stained glass: black,
indigo. The subtle markings of brief life. Together
with people who will one day leave each other
in a certain order. At dawn the first bird speaks,
thinks of nothing but day. The dream it drags
me away from. The one where I reverse off
a cliff and the car falls to its death but my body
is pulled by something unseen backwards through
the terror of air. The one where it just might be
the end for me. My husband asks what would
you rather know: when you will die or how
you will die? Either way, it's an awful
game. The black butterfly is a wish granter,
an omen of death, change, the passing of time,
good luck. The best sightings can mean
whatever you want them to. As I ate cheese
and dried apricots with my children last night
the robins formed a village army against
a marauding crow. Aerial bombs that in the end
could do nothing but protest. Their outrage
all volume and speed. The birds' baby my son
found dropped on our driveway. Its eyes still
blind. Black knobs. Its featherless quills.
Its frank yellow beak grimaced, but was the color of joy.

Monarch at the Telescope

The butterfly floats, ignores
the steel observatory dome
in a September blue as water.
Consider the orange and black
stained-glass of her wings.
How she won't stop, can't
stop to put her ommatidia
to the telescope eyepiece.

If she did, her omnivision
would show her a moon
like orbital bone. The eye socket,
pocket wrench metal, pitiless.
Instead, her proboscis
tends to a mud puddle that
could have pooled in a buried
pelvis. Her distracted mind.

She is like a scissor—
origami—as she beats
her hinged hips. Her wings slip
in delicious sky to join more
of her kind—a bivouac, a rusty
roost in the paralyzed cold
of her nights as she runs away
yes, to Mexico.

She has felt the loose dress
of childhood tighten against
her girth and she has fastened

her hook to an eye of milkweed
like an open air uterus, unzipped
from her exoskeleton like
an autopsy incision. Eaten
herself poisonous. She has

told me not to come near.
It seems like years she spent
never knowing that I'd be thinking of her
when I sit by the firepit poking at ashes—
an old door having burned away from a red-hot hinge.

I Want Milkweed Hair

I have put my trust in the indifference of wind.

Now is the moment of my most wise. I have failed to calm down.
Now I lie in hypnagogic state. I didn't defend myself.

The children are getting too old. I have eaten too much sugar.
This is when I should get hired for all the jobs.

When I was young I didn't listen. Failed to plant with knowledge of the sun,
soil, or water, but saw the old women's parachutes glow

for a week in autumn—
their cottony heads, candy glistening in the bottom of a purse.

Wind sent them tumbling, snagging against brown
detritus of leaves, lives of loved ones.

I want their hair.
I defended myself. Daughter to a peacekeeper.

Their white silk bounced,
in little laughing bundles

bounded across the earth,
didn't need to ask for help.

I am a milkweed pod split open—
nine hundred silk-white hairs attached to my seeds.

Messages

The porch light shining on my bedroom ceiling
means my son isn't home yet and the clock
glows an hour I used to rock him in my arms
with the stealth of a woven web.

Mom, I need some advice, he texts.
Should I date someone new?
His ex-boyfriend still holds him too closely.
I encourage him to go for it. Ask him
what he's afraid of. His version of afraid
is different from mine.

In the morning I listen to true crime,
walk straight into the dark woods. Going from sun
to shade creates an optical portal,
and I approach seeking its message.

The oval frame of hemlock needles glitters green.
A bug lands on my arm. A spider works its web.
The sun slants, spotlights the silken
cable—a highway between the living and the dead—
a tree with ferns growing out of its upturned
roots. My eyes adjust and I hear messages in mycelia,

secrets the woods don't know are secrets.
Every busy thing, shadowed or spotlit. A son
who embraces the night the way a bat navigates
the spaces between hazards. Who used to
be so close to the floor he could rest his head

on the cat, his stuffed gorilla, his friend, anything
he loved that he could show his love to. I was the
milk, the kindness, the snug hip. He was piloting
black sky—a ship, newborn and polished as wet stone.

Essex Serpent

There, I held you in the lake as you fell asleep against my legs. You had armor on. I could see the skin at the base of your neck. I picked at a scar there. We spun around in the water the way one can in the water. You, weightless but pulling. Me, dizzy and watching the waves churn. One of the water splashes became a hand waving. At me. I reached for it, pulled it towards me. It was our son. I hadn't met him before, but knew it was our son by the shape of his lips. As if I had nursed him as a baby. We spun around and around. You said to him, "Did they give you legs?" He couldn't get out of the water. I was both myself and him at the same time. The only being I wasn't, was you. And you left me in the water. My legs behind me. Useless. Glad I didn't have to get out of the water. Didn't want you to see my legs. I stayed there, hovering, held up by my arms on the shore like the first amphibian, and watched you go.

The Feeling of History

I swam with cartoon fish when I fell in the Herring Run.
Drawings of the Revolutionary War made my body feel strange. Like their

muskets were fictions firing. They weren't photos after all.
The sun on the west coast looks wan to me in photos. I haven't

seen enough rainbows. In my dream I'm walking on a beach.
Pass the body of a dead girl. Maybe she's sleeping. Either way,

in the dream no one cares. We want to attain those cliffs
on the horizon. The ones where clouds cling to the land

like illustrations in history books. When I wake I find
myself in horror. I read faces. I can sing, but I don't always know

the words. Prefer to be alone for long stretches. In my dream
we aren't human. Why aren't we human? This morning after

the sleet storm, animals have left wayward tracks.
I wonder why there are rabbits in winter.

You'd think they'd go underground before it got cold. They're
like little singers on snowbank stages. Bolt away at the slightest

sound. Their tracks are like histories, aimless and insignificant.
So easily erased by the next storm. The little feet that came

right up to my door left a mystery. There aren't any tracks leading away.
Whose powerful wings took it off its feet? Or did someone let it in?

Hibernal Night Photo: A Foggy Park in Snow

This is menopause. Amniotic fluid stewed.
Roof rot, hanging clot. Hemming

and hawing. The precise moment brews,
spreads, broods over years—contradicts—

smears blood on months of cloths
pages upon pages. My lot.

Little did I know. In December
the river's tidal nightsweat

soups up, breaks its own numb banks.
Hum and buzz of ice on which

I've seen a seal glissade, but now
it's twilight the lamplight's switched on.

Memory shambles down
the tunneled path. I hate to double back.

There's this blue tinge and pink halo.
A crepuscular corona lisps its light,

murmurs in the murk. What should be
sharp spectrum, all ice-pick, pinprick stars

becomes instead a fog-balm warmth—
an abomination. I discern (as if static

could be seen) what might be a pine tree
but through the haze a woman skulks.

Her hair dulls to a milky egg—face
flushed to the roots as fiery as a fox tail glows.

Against Regret

> *"The moon has nothing to be sad about,/Staring from her hood of bone.//*
> *She is used to this sort of thing./Her blacks crackle and drag."*
> —Sylvia Plath, "Edge"

In case of emergency, give a perfunctory nod. Yes,
there is nothing to be sad about. Walk the line
between horizon and telephone wire. Resemble
a traveling figure from antiquity. Mercury
in cracked leather pausing to wash his face in a creek.
Become smaller than you were once. Seen
from far away. The distance of water spans
your selves. Oh, your hood covers your greasy hair
like a snood. Your hair itches and tangles
in the birches. You're not fleeing. No pursuits.
You'd think the weights you carry would break you,
but you'll die putting on socks and new sweaters.
You've made the mistakes of your father.
Against regret. Snows are heavier wet. When
the landscape's black and white snatches color
it is the sky that comes back to rescue you.
You'll be buried under your quilt as if it is dirt
and the sun will resurrect what yellows you crave.

Dearest,

It was snowing when we drove you to the airport. Today the sun shines that you've landed in London. Your nerves jangled the night before, you sent me a story you wrote called "A Little Secret" in which your plane was crashing over the ocean. In it, you implore Death to keep its secrets to itself and let you have a little fun. How this introduced me to your primal fears.

Today I wonder how the red grapes in my mouth got all the way to New Hampshire from Peru. How in the photos you're sending, the old architectures shine, slick and glowing gray with sunshower. Stand alongside the new buildings' mirrored crusts. I wonder how it's humanly possible to track where you stand on this earth just by looking at my phone.

Along with all the old wonders you're sending—cobblestone streets, cracked leather of pubs—I can look out my own window and see the birds that flit to my porch ceiling, never stopping long enough to identify. Pilots use instruments to see where they're going in a storm. A passenger's trust opens in the palms. In the slack drunk mouth.

Yesterday morning at the Boston hotel, I wondered why there weren't more birds than airplanes flying. How the eye tracks the white bird as it avoids slamming skyscraper windows. How the moon's white mouth mentioned the seagull's feathers. You'd think it would have sounded muffled. But it came to my ears as a sharp and cold atmosphere. We were falling from the 38th floor.

We're both on the ground. Your day has gotten ahead of you, ahead of us here at home. You're in photos with Big Ben under the night sky. Our moon last night was full. Though I couldn't see the object, it shone blue in this house of your birth.

III.

Dear Morpheus

This morning I didn't take the time
to linger in your message. Would you
please send it again? I want to feel
the edges of your dream-bricks,
the way morals take no part
in what happens there. I've found
love where there was none, lost
people to future events. When I'm
drowsy please let me read your letters.
I've had to watch as the TV forms
nuanced portraits of concern and doubt.
Contained ships of grief. Bubbles
of pink spew and grassy hills that tirade
their muddy haunches across my hips.
I want to get out and sever the neck
off a champagne bottle. Spray the hull
of the ship with my celebration. Want
to gasp and fever match a chess game.
A chest game? Perhaps with longing
you can come to me, confess everything.
I will listen to what you know. Give me
original tangerines and marvelous
puppets with invisible strings. Kites
to clouds and rivers that rise up
with hand-drawn dramas. I'd love
to know what you know. Why you
take your time to show me the dead
as if they're right in front of me. Versions
of life and those tactile sounds they make.
Show me why I can't have the loves I have.

Incubus

In my dream I ate lettuce so green and crispy I drooled. I swallowed the demon in its folds and went back to visit my old apartment. On the porch the screen door looked so vivid I opened it to make sure it still slammed to satisfy. The sound brought me back so hard. I'd offer money to take that screen door home. I thanked the occupants for not kicking me out. They let me look for my bedroom but instead I found a whole new building like an annex. Man did I miss that screen door's smack. Beyond the door I could see the sky was turning pink over the river. It was so lush and hidden in plain sight. Behind me were the clocks and a telephone. I felt them there but didn't see. The demon I had choked down could make me orgasm at the sight of a slick sky. I bucked against the pain of that remembered door's slam.

The brown house that can kill you

won't allow the lights to stay on. You flip the switch and the house snatches the light into shadow. The phone call from your mom crackles and disconnects. She's been talking for a year about cleaning the house in preparation for her death. Whatever you do, don't fall asleep in bed. This is the house where your dreaming self stays. Even when you're awake it exists, like an attic of the mind. You think of it before you fall asleep, hoping to dream of it again. Maybe this time you'll find the architect. It's a mansion really. With back stairs that lead to that other wing. That bedroom you've never seen before. That annex of possibility. The chimney that's also an exit but will only act as an entrance. It wounds you. The magic house can feel like being birthed, but will definitely kill you. Your childhood house had attic stairs behind a door. You were terrified of what might be up there. Once, you had sleep paralysis and a bat flapped helplessly into the room, landed on your chest and you were stone. Inert as a sheet of paper as the bat twitched on your breastbone. Your breath is gone. Summer air breathes through the open windows. Everything is moving except you. Is this what it is to die with things left undone?

Intentions

I sit down at my kitchen table with my intentions
after a long absence. They have come to the door
after I notice my lack of visitors. Our friendship

is based on luck, wild hairs, and cruel fate. I open
my heart and receive a smattering of praise, suture
my chest as I sign all of our old contracts in blood.

We are reconciled, have tea in cups crusted
with inscrutable predictions. The dishwasher has failed
to do its one job and I still can't read signs.

When my intentions are angry, they arrive
unannounced in my dark bedroom, shake me awake
with a violent hand on my shoulder.

Crushing my clock, they mock my need for sleep.
I cower in agreement, nodding my head yes.
I raise my arms, protecting my face from blows.

Going to work, I avoid them in my car, veering
around them as if they are two crows eating roadkill,
their folded wings opening in escape.

Disoriented at 2 AM

Are you on drugs? Can you hear the cigarette sizzle as you inhale?
Do you come to and find yourself stuck in marsh mud?

Is someone chasing you? Have you injected
fentanyl that zombifies your arms?

Are you a lab rat? Did you step on a wasp nest?
Have you cringed at the holes? The black/yellow bodies?

Who idles in the pickup in the strip club parking lot?
A windowless building painted matte black as a knife hilt.

Have you started smoking again? Are you hooked
on the rush and the crush of smoke in the throat?

Where do you tie off your arm? Is it a porch overlooking
the train tracks? Are the screens torn? Stained mattress on the floor?

Do you even have a dim bulb? When did you tell yourself
just this once? How many times ago was that?

When was your last dream from a safe place? Is all that's left of you
a skeleton? Your jeans ripped off and your flip phone open to a dead 911 call.

Birth Story

I was watching myself give birth
in the dream as if it were a movie.
A man I knew talked and talked.

Said *breathe out before you push*
instead of *breathe before you push*
I knew how to do it right, but I listened to him.

I said *her head is out.*
I saw myself squatting
on a rock with her head crowning,

then the baby was placed
on the pine tree bough
I used to make mud pies under as a child.

She was covered in mud and balanced
like a leopard asleep.
I had no fear she'd fall.

Her lips turned first before her head
as infants do towards the breast
but there was only a branch.

She peeled its bark off
between her lips.
How did I push her out?

I found the power of my breath
but not until her life was at stake.
She would not emerge until my voice became fire.

Art School Accepted Students Day

In my dream I found her old retainer on the basement floor. Awake, I know why. Because now her teeth are straight but she worries they are still crooked. She is grown and growing.

What do I know about when daffodils should flower? Crocuses' resilience doesn't excite me this spring. Their talent's wasted. Their frigid torment. Brief as candle wax. Sad as a sculpture constructed of baby teeth.

And on my walk along the river, the seal lounges on the dock while locals point their cameras at his flippers. Full of sea lamprey—fish that look like eels and have horrifying horned teeth—he applauds himself.

My daughter's sketch of a vase brings me to tears. The ellipse at the mouth. The confident charcoal. A vessel that could hold water. How it feels to be a made thing and crying my praise.

Dream Cinema

I'd like to see them come up with
a cinema for my dreams. Watch honeysuckle syrup
and cats climbing the bedpost. Its
character riding a bicycle at night lying down.
Setting: the turning sky. The humid stars.
The treetops whizzing past. All my paths I ever forgot.
For once on screen in all their mundane
insanity. It'll be like I made my own meaning.
Who else cares about my themes? It's their debut
and they're wearing it best. Yes, it will be
a documentary. Surreal, but what facts
aren't these days? My neighbor says
It's like walking kites to describe her
three dogs on leashes. When I watch myself
drive the car from the backseat I'll come up
with similes too. Find myself in another
country with no way back
to the airplane. All those doors of bronze
reliefs and carved mahogany. The paint
peeled back to reveal. Who I'd get to see again.
Those who've died and those who've simply
left my life. Bit parts and starring roles.
Those people whose names are household
and the extras I'll never see again. Maybe
it's just their hands I've noticed. Serving
the coffee I can't drink before spilling.
What would I contribute there? In the theater
of my dreams I'd sleep and sleep. Make more
movies for the waking. The tears I can do nothing
to stop. The throat bunched. The voice
slumped over the steering wheel.

The Aubergine Dress

I stood in a gallery of another woman's house reading out loud from an aubergine dress. The dress was her poem, not mine. Each tier of the chiffon skirt needed translation. *The bodice encircles the heart. Lines stitched into circles of skirt. Stanzas the storeys of a house. Body of a woman, the form.* The woman wearing it was dark purple, her face a port-wine stain. She had neglected to tell me about the fish in her indoor pool. Hungry, it came out of the filter but I didn't know what to feed it. Bread? Fish flakes? The pale goldfish swam in the air above the water and I pet its muscled back as it moved through my hand. It wasn't a bird or a cat. It was still a fish. Too late (for the woman had left), I asked the dress, *where's the fish food?* I was taking care of her home while she was away. *Everyone out of the pool* I said, and dashed through the cement corridors of the compound searching for the stash in vacant stores. The fish was good for the house. Night fell. The bright conical skirts of security lights came on, lit the shadowed portico. Houseguests mumbled drunk in their sleep. The woman had left her dress empty. I was afraid of changing my life.

Rabbit Nest Beneath the Snapdragons

Their mother made her final visit during last
night's thunderstorm. Lightning made the babies
scream. The nest flooded in my mind.

Scribbled on the insides of my eyelids
the day wakes me. If I let the light in
the dream fades. I breathe on the dream's glass,

peer in on my pride. My teacher
said mine was her favorite, but my classmates
wouldn't listen to my story through their chatter.

My words on the page were unfamiliar
as if I hadn't been their author. All the
chairs emptied save the jealous one.

Outside the classroom, fear occupied every landing
of the descending stairs. My legs were not attached
to my feet with any meaning but tried to run.

I've never wanted to plunge to the ground floor
faster than when that disturbed mind pursued me.
Now I am awake, the babies have gone.

Fairy Ring

I've got eagle eye, fish eye, cat's eye lenses.
A nitpicker, I scan the milkweed
for pupae. Think on how to save
what I can save. The headline shrieks:
some climate change effects may be irreversible
and consider throwing myself
in front of a train just to reduce
carbon emissions. These thoughts
fill my own landfill called
the dump for useless worry.
The wasp nest in the entryway.
The dead mouse collecting flies.
The bills stamped in red: Past Due.
Which alarm do you press first?
The squirrels wouldn't care if we
disappear, they can eat mushrooms.
Mushrooms don't need us. The house
would fall to them eventually. Their
fairy rings like every dream I can't
remember. If you step inside
one you will be forced to dance
until you die from exhaustion.
When I fly away I'll be able
to see everything. Won't need a coat
anymore. I'll watch myself
push off the ground
as if I'm in a swimming pool
tended to by someone else.
The dreams will finally find the lost
cats. The folded papers will
unfold. All our soaked words
swim into view. Narratives to un-tell.

Recurring

You are standing in front of the house again. The high fence around it. Only the garret is visible. This time it has windows. You know you shouldn't go inside. *Is this intuition?* Sleep tries to remind you. Your eyes flick back and forth beneath thin lids. Someone might watch them flutter, wondering what you're scanning. You're inside the house now. You shouldn't be here. There's a room you shouldn't go inside, levels and stairs. A rabbit warren. Here is the sunken living room. Here is the teenager's bedroom with posters on the walls. Dread settles in your bones a dark brown wood. This is an architect's home. The dead come back to berate you for your crimes. Absolve you of guilt. The dead mother lives with her husband and his new wife. She rolls her eyes. You hold her shoulder. *Don't go in the room that feels wrong.* Intuition is hard to hear against the pulsing breath of the room behind the door. You're absurd being human, absurd being a trespasser. You know the house cannot burn.

In a dream of what-ifs

I'm the only one left
on earth. The waves
have all gone home.
The mountains are trees
with awkward smiles.
Majestic springs screwed
and bowlegged as a singer's
signature. Poof. I'm
falling through the spermy
air. Cars are empty. Care
is a white stripe in black hair
at the microphone. Baby,
I'm on my own. The last
in a book of matches.

The night we all had insomnia

our bodies felt the roll of the tundra
the smell of the snow on our lips
the breath in the mitochondria

of all our histories
and roiled with traumas of the belly
the breaking of the stomach open

to the sky in half-sleep
the vulnerable soft body
the way the air gets colder

when the partner leaves
the way the air is always getting older
golder and heavier with sorrow

the pillow and its stars
the tears it's kept and is keeping hidden
secret like any trapdoor in a mystery

we can't wait to watch unfold but clench
our toes against the terror
the way any person holds themselves

protects the rib cage
trying to fall away as if
into bright air or coffee-dark dirt

the roots sticking out and brushing
the elbows as we plummet
the light in the hole above us

gets smaller until it winks out
and our rabbit bones are left
with little fur on the heels

the grass we ate in summer
the snow under our long feet
so unlucky and unlikely to repeat the year

the same way twice
or make it to a third
while all our longing and decisions

make a nest underground
dead grass and leaves and the softest fur
only predators dream to peel away and eat

we are so hungry for what leaves us
what has left us but also what won't leave
as if it's food and we can't live

unless we chew on that green worry
until we can no longer taste
we are so full of chlorophyll and the world ends

in the dream of making our dead come back
haven't we all seen the peculiar hop
of that kind of animal awake in the dark

Wounds vs. Wounded

The surgeon gave your core four punctures.
You try to hug but I hold my body away

to protect your wounds. A couple of hours
mended the tear in your abdominal wall

where your intestine poked through. Drugged,
you act like you've never been cut open before.

In your recovery you fight against sleep's
weakness however strong its hold. How

this is your metaphor for being
male. I've never seen anyone willingly

transform. The way you have stood outside
yourself and looked. A real piece of work

takes work. And you've taught me. Grateful
for these mountain rocks. These children

we've made who pick their way up the slippery
boulders. Their ankles firm against the white rush

of mountain runoff. The waterfall's cold
against their faces. I've convinced them

they need to feel to be alive. Alive? Yes,
they are alive in their skin. Their wounds

invisible to any untrained eye in seeing past
a well-trained smile. Smiles and lies. I have

buried those old penetrations. Eaten them.
I've breathed them like oxygen for so long

the mask has left marks on my cheeks.
You want to press closer to me. I want you to heal.

Nocturne

You're asleep upstairs while I eat green grapes.
The mystery I'm watching dulls their pop
as I bite down, squeeze the juice, and swallow.
I've wiped the sticky remote, and cleared
the people from my day. Leading men
act like toddlers. Spit their anger instead
of swallowing it. Shed tears but won't say
why. Their women forgive. He throws a chair
against his demons, but still solves the crime,
gets the girl even though she's dead.
Even the living ones long for him.
I climb the stairs I'll need to vacuum soon, enter
the bedroom in considerate stealth.
Predict how hot I'll get. Go to bed, where thoughts
drip from a broken faucet even in the comfort
of the clean sheets I put on today. The pillow
forgives. The mattress pushes into my knee.
Sometime in the night, I wake and wonder
if you're even there, the bed's gone so cold.
My nightshirt's soaked through. Awakened by a fire
in the forest I'm lost inside. Huddled
in a pile of dead leaves, my arms hug bent legs,
my forehead rests on my knees.

On the Eve of the Last Lunar Eclipse of 2021

—after Plath's "The Rival"

This afternoon I surprised the moon
its mouth in the shape of an O
as if it realized it still loves me.
Just before night hatted its head,
bald and age-spotted as a spouse,
before the clouds' wool blanketed
its widened eyes. And why should
it be different each time it arrives?

This time it's a fixed ball punched by wind.
The next, it glows in borrowed yellow
against horizon's daylight-pink.
As if this light was something new.
An idea. A sunk coin glinting. Winter
is coming. There will be moonless nights
flickering with glitter. Starlight cold
shimmering like a desert mirage.

Our passing each year spins
faster and faster. The pace
we can't outrun. But still I'm enthralled
by each transformed face.
Tonight as we sleep, I'll feel the sun
of my husband's warmth and by morning
the moon will have spent the night
eclipsed by earth's blood-red umbra.

Discord in Marriage

Now when I go out the river breaches
its banks and fills the street to the knees
and the cold winter water seeps
while anger recedes like a house
in a rearview mirror. To a vanishing
point but still it sputters and flares
like a guttering candle tricking
and drawing me back. The pavement
dips with the sunken earth sinkhole
and the train tracks yield heat
after the bulk of it passes. Enough
to squeeze a coin like molten glass
through a press's cylinder. So hot
to boil milk at its clang.

After Reading "Walking Around" by Pablo Neruda

The moon was never promised
to be yellow. The sheep never green.
I was told and so I left that wrong
answer behind. Corrected.
I am tired of being so domestic. In service.
Like the kitchen countertops, knife-nicked
and loosened from the frame. Lift me
and see everything kept in my drawers.
The plastic and the glinting cutlery. There
is stickiness left by everyone else. It's in
the treads of my shoes. Underneath
my fingernails. What I want to do is walk
and dance. Why can't people feel my
rhythm? People will think I'm a lunatic.
Gesturing at the air. Galloping. My hair
decorated with a tattered napkin. My garbage
will be treasures left in small mousy places.
On my walks I see the brick walls
and birds who don't like me at all. The river water
that falls faster now that it's rained a torrent.
I go into the jewelry shop and pick up
my resized wedding ring. The gold looks
newer after. I could bite it like a chocolate bar
with the wrapper on. I remember
wearing it for the first time. How it looked
against the tan beach sand and the blue
of sky. How the water glittered. The five
sapphires spun out in my eyes. I am tired
of the coffee stain that has promised me
it would be cleaned. The alarm promised

me it would wake. I am tired of everything
but the things I have yet to do. Things
I'll wait to do until I come home
and no one is there. No car in the driveway.
No dish to wash but my own favorite
coffee mug. One plate. One fork and spoon.
What I want to do versus what I actually do.
My rage is not nearly as strong as others'.
Why I always find the river so mighty
the rocks disappear. The spice of ground
peppercorns puts me in a room with oil paint.
The scent of a bookstore puts me in mind
of telling a friend what happened to make me so sad.

Gratitude List

At bedtime I make a list of ailments   body parts that hurt   at night I wake
myself with a full body lunge away from the nightmare abductor coming
at me through that thin dissolving membrane   at dawn I wonder what
color the sky is   at ten I thought *double digits*   at once I must combine all
I've consumed and form it like clay   at my desk I put my head down and
sob   at school my teacher would turn out the lights and make us put our
heads down   at school I longed   at dinner   at church   at home   was I ever
in charge at all   at times I was seven and scared   at other times I was 18 and
looking over my shoulder   at bedtime I make a list of gratitudes   stuff the
headphones in my ears against anyone's noises   at my own noise   the gears
in my head   at my friend's house we listened to music and   at the pond we
smoked   at lunch we gathered in the courtyard   at bedtime I make a list of
ailments   at the top of my head   at the bottom of my feet   at no time am I
ever   at no time am I ever   at once old and young and   at bedtime I make a
list of gratitudes leaking in like music that won't die   at the hooks that dig
in and sing until I'm sick with it   at night I leak like music   at church   at
the dance   at memory   at all at all at all

Grounding Method

Eagles are big enough without my dreams
making them into giants. In that space even
I note how strangely they blot out the sun.

Today the temperature rose fifty degrees
and the snow melts in one giant tragedy into
the earth. The way blackbirds fell

from the sky by the hundreds in Mexico
yesterday. Sometimes reality is more surreal
than anything I can dream. I'd love to live

on beauty and love. Safety and release.
A turkey vulture keeps coming around.
Its seesawing wings tip. High winds

toss the black outline. Something must
be dead in the neighborhood. And it hovers,
glides. In dreams, I'll never outrun my fears.

I keep running to the window to look,
as if my eyes can be trusted to verify
what I've already identified as survival.

I am here. I just am. Name a stomach where I
can rest my hand. Name myself blameless.
Think of my favorite flavor. Smell my way home.

V.

When Asked How I Will Begin

I will begin with my body.
How it lifts me away
from the floor even as it
holds me to the ground.
My feet will make contact first.
Then air fills me. My chest
barely navigates the words
not spoken. The breath heaved
from sleep. I will begin
with water. Washing a face.
Emptying my body of waste.
Filling its cavern. What if
I was fire? Today I would
make the flame rise higher.
Today I would find
what matters by what burns.
Feet begin to flame
as the end of day weighs on.
The furnace is down there.
Underneath the trapdoor.
The fireplace flickers. A painting
of water above the mantel
curves its way into leaving.
Thorns catch clothing as I go.
I have been breathing air all day.
I will begin the end with fire.
Hold it in my palms. The night
will part with my going. Close
behind me like velvet
in a darkened theater.

Winter Solstice at Daybreak

Early to the party she lends me her robes,
her candy and matches,
lights the dome with dyed pastel streaks—
the fluff of watered-down blood
and the crunch of an heirloom egg.
Her hair lies strewn across the morning pillow,
wavy with the bent crush of sleep.
If I borrowed her flavors,
the temperature I'd dress myself with would
be sub-zero, even with her friendly smile
that reaches the power lines
crosshatched against her chest.
She's either a captive or fine art.
The eye now opening beyond a dream
turns away from radical beauty
and towards the mundane. No longer
this baby light, a novelty
that brought my face a flush,
she's weaker now a minute's passed.
Her strains of music wanly leak. The song
cannot penetrate all the opening
eyes behind the wheels of cars, garbage cans,
and even toy trucks pushed by tiny imaginations
that salt the earth against the perils of winter.

Visitor

I can hear the tree workers next door chainsawing the old limbs. Even the shower can't drown it out. I stay in extra long. Today I need to burn the cold out of me. There's this knot in my throat as if I'm pinewood. There's this failing that can't be swallowed. I've been remembering old facts of my childhood. Things that haven't stayed in fashion. Crocheted ponchos. My mother's punch bowl and a ladle for serving. The bundt pan ice disk floating like a lifesaver in a miniature pool. The sweet bubbles she concocted. I'm looking at my daughter's chaotic bedroom thinking I could make it into art. Her body I'm responsible for assembling is neat as a pin. Sharp contrast to her crumpled clothing mixed in with garbage. How she numbs herself against the knife edge of life. I'm remembering my father rolling a newspaper and lighting the kindling in the fireplace. His shoehorn and tin of brown Kiwi shoe polish. His tie collection. My mom's grid method for transferring an image. Carbon paper. Her green speckled case of pencils. I'm imagining what a good parent does these days. I turn away from the mildewed ceiling. Let the hot water pelt my eyes. Wonder why this balled up fist showed up today on the doorstep of my throat. I recognize the feeling. Its fingerprints clenched, a fist inside like a trees' concentric rings.

To My Sky in Winter

You make no apology. Even though I beseech you
to acknowledge what I'm going through. The abuse

of stinging sleet. The lonely way you mock me. And I'm still here
standing under you. Making the choice to stay and walk the river.

Every reflection lords you over me. My stick breaks the ice.
You are the bird's sidewalk. Do you need each other?

Who am I to say we're done? I can't blast off without you.
Without you, neither can I taste the berries of summer.

So you've given me heat, that's our history. You can take it
away too. Prod me awake with your desire. Where I am

on the planet in December is cold. Even gloves take degrees
away from my blood. I'm a radiator against my will.

Your apology always comes too late. I am so wretched
I forgive you your temperament. Turn my face up to your changes.

Though you've buried my heart in drifts of snow,
your hand on my back is warm, meant no harm.

This Feeling in March

Robins clog a thawed patch of scraggly grass. Six raw meat-colored breasts clot inside a circle of snow.

Once small enough for me to hold the whole of them, my children have grown to ever-widening territories. Wolves or lone cats, they spray their scent on the voyage out, then return.

I caught the bleary eye of morning, red and sweet as corn syrup blood.

Her eyes when she's crying ovals of pain.

Worked in woe I have no more tears. Can't conjure them even with magic.

Steeped in patience I've waited out my sentence. This sentence ends but is transfigured the way transitions mark the space between bodies that once touched.

I named them.

She is beautiful goddess. She is pearl. Youthful and downy. Razored sear of lightning.

He is gracious. God is. Smiles easy as a temperate sun.

When the year moves away from the first month, I can feel it stalking me beneath the blinding snow. What I know of it I can count on again.

Slit of menthol green in an otherwise blue sky. February light. A chlorine pool foreseen.

Shadowed, trees cast themselves out as the nets of fishermen. Slide their slow tendrils over the drifts. I'm upended.

A cat's white belly mirrors the surface of snow. His back gray as today's sky. In the river, the great blue heron's chest feathers dangle like icicles in the moonscape of thawing ice.

I'm going to start painting my children. Their eyes in daydream, hands deep in the cat's fur, or maybe they'll be palm up, bringing me their gifts.

Cartography

I get my test results in spring.
         In spring the freezing rain spits its memories of winter.
Winter found me flying, trying to flee and forget.
         Forgetfulness came easier than expected. I'd hoped
hope would see me from the earth.
         The earth was so small the plane's window revealed
revelations like a nameless map. Was that where I'd ever been before?
         Before place I had always had myself.
My *self*. No matter where I was
         I was this brain. Eyes on stalk-like legs walking around.
Around the nerves of what I learned.
         Learning by seeing what makes my arteries different.
Differentiate between the fenestration of my vein.
         This vein I'll call my poetic artery.
Artery made odd in the making, in the womb.
         Womb, a word which comes from belly, bowels, heart, uterus.
Uterine anomalies in fibroid tumors like freckles said all the doctors.
         Doctor of poetry, I see the terrain of my body.
Body snapshotted, mapped with the eye of an X-ray.

March

It's March and the image of the wind
is a man breathing from the sky.

His is a cloud-shaped head. Blue
and black and white fills the outline.

It's March and I'm biding my time.
If the air could just release me. I'm prone

in the bed dreaming of a shirt hanging
on a line. I'm prone to fits of anxiety.

Any boiled water I drink comes bubbling
to the skin like shame. I'm learning

to throw water on it before it rages.
I was just burning something in the yard

and the whole county caught fire. Mud
seeped in and clogged the pipes.

Nothing works anymore. Machinery
doesn't think. Like me it keeps chugging along.

The sun is leaving striped shadows.
The snow has been dazzling for so long

the landscape is starting to bore me.
I can't fashion a response to this weakness

in my eyes. Can't say I'm not impatient
for the season to hurry up and change.

But I'm putting my hand up telling it *stop*.
Someone told me they saw the first crocus.

Its purple petals sharp and curved. I heard
people talking about the witch hazel appearing

and there it was. From my kitchen window
I see pussy willows. When I was little I'd stroke

them against my face and wish they'd turn
into brand new kittens that would stay small forever.

Instructions for Life's Terrible Wonder

Wake up with an opinion. Broadcast it. Want someone to hear it. Fear they will kill you. Take a walk and witness a kettle of turkey vultures soaring over. Wonder if you are dead and just don't know it. Look around for evidence you are alive. Find there are no more humans. Decide if this is heaven, its March winds are uncomfortable. Realize you are dressed for it at least. Name the vultures the twelve disciples. Hope that here in heaven, none of the same needs tug at your sleeve as they did in life. Haul resentment to the landfill. Take note of evening coming on, the low, moody rain clouds holding onto their grudge. Decide responsibility means only that you have to look and let light shine through you. Make sure this moment stays in your mind. Remember the wholesome yellow glow shining from someone's window, the rush of snowmelt on the river. Absolve all debts you think you're owed. Keep unsolved the cold case of your Love. Laugh at the wonder of this heaven on earth.

October's End

Just as I'm starting out I'm landing.

I dart and stick, vibrate and spasm like a struck squirrel.
Stay safe on a branch as it sways in the storm—

Wild turkeys and wet trees.
Wind's whining beats the black width of bald eagle wings.

Peripherally, they're brief leaves—
panicked and alone, the last yellow on a branch

that seesaws down, edge a blade.
When windows in a house are its eyes

they soothe me. Glass and panes reflect and reveal.
Oh yes, something hunted hangs from my mouth—

Rain fogs my glasses. No one sees me cross.
Pine needles like pick-up sticks. A great blue heron

in the field, looked at twice.
My hips loose as hunter's gunfire. The deer launch at dusk.

Something's left a foreleg dangling from a tree. Its hoof
struck dumb and gnawed in the air—a last leap.

Acknowledgements & Thanks

Thank you to the editors of the following journals and anthologies in which these poems first appeared:

Book of Matches: "Discord in Marriage"

Broadkill Review: "In a dream of what-ifs," "Worm Moon"

The Disappointed Housewife: "Mystery Speaks"

Eunoia Review: "Art School Accepted Students Day," "Cartography," "Disoriented at 2AM," "Intentions," "She-Hulk," "Wounds vs. Wounded"

Gone Lawn: "The Aubergine Dress," "Essex Serpent," "lover lover over and over"

Gyroscope Review: The Crone Power Issue, "I Want Milkweed Hair"

Gyroscope Review: "Ouroboros"

Hamilton Stone: "After Reading 'Walking Around' by Pablo Neruda"

Hole in the Head Review: "Monarch at the Telescope"

Impossible Task: "Say Memories are Current Events," "When You Start Running at 51," "When Asked How I Will Begin"

Lily Poetry Review: "Dear Morpheus"

Litro: "Incubus"

The Mackinaw: "Gratitude List"

MacQueen's Quinterly: "The brown house that can kill you"

Menacing Hedge: "Against Regret," "As Ann Darrow," "One Hundred Percent Effaced"

Mom Egg Review: "Visitor"

Mom Egg Review Summer / Girl – A Literary Folio: "The Elephant's Child"

Moss Puppy Magazine: "Gizzard Brain," "Recurring"

Neologism Poetry Journal: "You Can Catch More Flies with Honey than with Vinegar"

The Night Heron Barks: "Hibernal Night Photo: A Foggy Park in Snow"

On the Seawall: "Messages"

One Art: "Purple"

Radar Poetry: "The night we all had insomnia"

Ran Off with the Star Bassoon: "I like to ride on things that shouldn't be ridden"

River Run Anthology: "March," "To My Sky in Winter," "There is Nothing Not with me Anymore," "This Feeling in March," "Winter Solstice at Daybreak"

Scissors & spackle: "Grounding Method," "Sometimes you wake from unnerving dreams"

South Florida Poetry Journal: "What the Red-Spotted Purple Butterfly Brought"

Speckled Trout Review: "Sleeping Over for the First Time"

SurVision: "Birth Story"

Thirteen Myna Birds: "Know-It-All"

—

Thank you to City Hall Poets for your keen eyes and longtime support. Not to mention your friendship. Also, thank you to Tresha Faye Haefner and The Poetry Salon poets. These poems would literally not exist without you. My gratitude goes out to judge Marsha de la O and Gunpowder Press editors for this honor. Thank you to my students who are always teaching me. To my parents: thank you for your example, and your support and encouragement which has made these words alive.

Jessica Purdy lives in coastal New Hampshire with her family. Her poems have appeared in *Action, Spectacle, About Place, On the Seawall, Radar, Gone Lawn, SoFloPoJo*, and elsewhere. She received her MFA from Emerson College. She has been a finalist for the Two Sylvias Press Wilder Poetry Book Prize, Action, Spectacle Book Prize, Codhill Press' Guest Editor Poetry Series, Granite State Poetry Prize, and Dryden-Vreeland Book Prize. She is the author of five books of poetry including her chapbook *The Adorable Knife: Poems based on The Nutshell Studies of Unexplained Death* (Grey Book Press) which received the NH Writers' Project People's Choice Award. Her other books include *STARLAND* and *Sleep in a Strange House* (Nixes Mate Books) which was a New Hampshire Literary Award for Poetry finalist. She teaches Creative Writing at SNHU and at Noble High School in North Berwick, Maine.